Foreword

The poems you'll discover within the following pages are a privileged peek into military life: a rare opportunity to listen to real people talking about their experiences in the forces. Poems by veterans, serving personnel and members of Army Cadets - as well as their families - shed light on the pride, elation and personal challenges of being associated with the military.

Life-changing events and significant moments (some monumental and others reassuringly day-to-day) are candidly captured in verse, leaving the reader with a much deeper understanding of what it means to serve.

I'm delighted that the proceeds from this charmingly illustrated book will support two very worthwhile charities: SSAFA, the Armed Forces charity and Sporting Force.

Enjoy!

Lorraine Kelly CBE.
TV presenter
National Honorary Colonel of the Army Cadet Force.

This book is dedicated to all those serving within the military, all those who have served and all those who paid the ultimate price for their Queen and Country.

Military Memories is proud to support the
following charities:

In support of:

The proceeds from this book will support SSAFA, the Armed Forces
charity.

Since 1885, SSAFA has been there to support those serving in our
Armed Forces, veterans and their families when necessary and in
order to restore their independence and their dignity.

SSAFA understands that behind every uniform is a person. And we
are here for that person – any time they need us, in any way they
need us, for as long as they need us.

In 2020 we supported over 79,000 people and we simply couldn't do
this vital work without the generosity of people like Gina, giving
her time and putting this wonderful book together.

Thank you, Gina and everyone who has contributed to this poignant
insight into military life from everyone at SSAFA.

In support of:

SPORTING FORCE
CREATE YOUR NEW LIFE

Sporting Force is a registered charity that has supported ex-service personnel, service leavers and reservists since 2015.

We offer ex-service personnel a route into civilian employment within the professional sports industry. Sports and coaching qualifications, training for other areas within the sports industry, work placements and employment support.

Sporting Force helps veterans and their families by offering social events to help relieve mental health and social isolation. All the opportunities we offer are inclusive and can be adapted to meet the needs of our veterans with disabilities.

Our wellbeing and fitness offer includes many sports, exercise and outdoor adventure activities. This brings camaraderie and being part of a team again, things that veterans all miss. We offer our services free of charge for all veterans and their immediate families.

PTSD and mental health challenges affect the whole family; we understand the pressures and pain involved. Making services open to partners of veterans and PTSD sufferers we offer access to support and opportunities for the families, an opportunity to meet others who understand what it's like to care for their loved ones, giving the opportunity to mutually support each other.

Special Thanks to...

Andy Jones - Illustrator
Hannah Slater - Graphic Designer
Patty O'Boyle - Advisor
Selina Cuff- Graphic Design and Publishing

Without these amazing people the book would not
have been possible.

Thank-you

Hello, and thank you for buying this book. This is a
collection of poems by veterans, serving personnel, families
of those who have served, and the wider Armed Forces family.

The poems illustrate the journey taken by those who join the
Armed Forces, showing the lighter side of our families' lives
and also the trauma we sometimes have to face.

Thank you

Gina Allsop, Editor
Veteran
Sergeant
Royal Corps of Signals

Our Journey

This is our journey
Memories written from the heart
From RAF, Army, Navy, and many volunteers.
But where did this all start?

It started with tragic loss:
A brother I will never forget;
Through a world of lockdowns,
Zoom meetings, weddings; and even funerals.

A poem of loss.
A charity too, that restores our faith in the human race.
A space to express emotions through verse, and the place
Our journey was born:
The military and its memories.

It's from the heart.
The impact can be sharp!
Our highs, our lows and our tales of woe.

We hope you enjoy the ebb and the flow.
We've a journey ahead, some miles to go
From signing on the dotted line
To conflicts far and wide in space and time.

Our journey, taken by many
Told by but a few:
We hope reading this may help inspire you.

Our Journey

Basic and Trade Training

Until Duty Calls

Sitting here alone, inside my four walls.
A global pandemic, a world on pause.
There's hard work ahead, for a just reward.
Just six weeks to go until duty calls.

A life on the road, so smooth until now.
Venues stand empty, where once there were crowds.
The band strikes up such a powerful chord,
How awesome it was to feel so adored.

Reflecting back on memories so fond,
Working with friends, so special a bond.
It's time to move on, a new life beckons.
I'll see them all soon; they'll miss me I reckon.

Preparing - still at home, inside these four walls.
Will this pandemic ever run its course?
The hard work begins, I'll give it my all.
Less than six weeks now, until duty calls.

Josh Betley
Recruit
Royal Marine Band Service

We're off to Join the Army

We wave goodbye at the station to family and friends,
Our bags are packed, keen to start our new lives in the green.
We're off to join the Army.
Our lives will never be the same again.

LEFT, RIGHT, LEFT shouts the corporal
Get in step!
LEFT, RIGHT, LEFT.

We meet our new family.
Our comrades, our new friends.
Were now in the Army.
Will we ever get to sleep a full night again?

LEFT, RIGHT, LEFT shouts the corporal
Necks in the back of the collar!
LEFT, RIGHT, LEFT

We learn to iron, polish and bull anything in our room.
Our kit all clean, gleaming and smart.
We are recruits in the Army;
Our job is to learn, learn, run, clean, and learn some more.

LEFT, RIGHT, LEFT shouts the sergeant.
Get on the back of your heels!
LEFT, RIGHT, LEFT

We learn how to kill the enemy.
Our bodies are fit and strong.
We are soldiers now.
Our Queen & country
We will serve till the end!

LEFT, RIGHT, LEFT shouts the RSM
EYES RIGHT!
LEFT RIGHT LEFT

Gina Allsop
Veteran
Sergeant
Royal Corps of Signals

No Joining Fee Today!

"You should join the British Army, lad. No joining fee today.
Just sign up on the dotted line and we'll pay you straightaway.
We'll teach you to be a soldier, lad, and train you in a trade,
So when you return to Civvy Street, your life will be well made."

And I thought of my life in the office, which was boring me insane,
Working for old Mr Humphreys, who holidayed in Spain.
And I thought of all the glory and I dreamed of all the fame,
And I signed up on the dotted line to the Sergeant's warm acclaim.

Soon I began my training, as a newly signed recruit.
They taught me how to press my kit, march smartly and salute.
Then after three months training, as the Corps Band proudly played.
On a cold December morning, was our passing off parade.

Mum and Dad stood there so proudly, as I marched on looking fine.
We did left wheel, then advanced to front and halted all in line.
The officer inspecting checked the turnout of each man,
Then climbed on the rostrum and his
stirring speech began.

"Every one of you looks splendid. You're an
honour to the Corps!
You'll soon begin trade training, then it
won't be long before
You're posted to your unit, which could be
in lands afar.
You'll have fun and travel widely, and soon
you'll have a car.

But you will never forget this day, you
became a soldier proud.
So congratulations, one and all, it's time
to cheer aloud.
Here's Hurray for the Royal Signals; then
we give our Queen "Hurray",
And a big "Hurray" for men like you, who we
honour on this day."
Then we marched off with our chests puffed
out and pulses beating fast,
And we met up with our Mums and Dads as the
Catterick wind blew past.

I have never felt so wonderful; I have never felt so good,
I will never feel that way again, and I guess I never should.

The recruiting sergeant had been quite right, when he told me of
the pay,
But what he didn't tell me of was the feeling of that day,
When you become a soldier, and learn a soldier's pride,
As you pass off one of the very best, with others at your side.

Clive Saunders
Veteran
Captain
Royal Corps of Signals

Improbable RAF Officer

First day at Cranwell; not a clue
Where to go or what to do?
Half the course calling themselves "ex rankers"
What a bunch of pretentious ... people.

I arrived without an ironing board
Their jaws were completely floored.
They caught each other's eyes,
Full of doubt
It was obvious I needed sorting out.

My lack of discipline was often contentious
But everyone helped, they weren't so pretentious.
"Right, come on! Let's get you sorted."
Turns out I was really well supported
I got there eventually.
Made incredible friends,
Turns out I helped them too, made amends.
It was tough but we got through together
And made some memories that I will cherish
forever.

So, what's next?
Four months on hold.
I'd never had it so good, truth to be told.
Lots of sport and loads of AT
I decided life on hold was the life for me.

Off to Shawbury for the air traffic course
Teach, train, reinforce.
Midweek nights out in "Shrews Vegas"
Taxis and DJs did quite hate us…

Then off to Leeming to control in the tower
Making time for the mess, especially happy hour
Cleared for take-off, cleared to land,
Learning my trade, practising first-hand.

Now I'm not so young, not so fresh-faced
Surrounded by children, no time to waste.
Wondering what the next chapter will bring
But I feel well prepared to face anything.

Neil Crosthwaithe
Flight Lieutenant
Royal Air Force

Sandhurst

The day you turn up is one you'll always remember,
Be it January, May or September.
You're greeted by staff then enter the Grand Entrance,
They tick people off, for us: 271 in attendance.

The rush then begins, to-ing and fro-ing,
The labyrinth of corridors is actually a test to become an officer…
Let's see if you actually know where you're going!

You meet your staff and then your parents say their goodbyes.
Family, partners and loved ones, some with tears in their eyes.
The intake then steps off and marches around Chapel Square,
Unbelievably, the day's just beginning - just so you're aware.

Hours blend into days and days into weeks.
The things that will elude you are the outside world and sleep.
Before you know it the Week 5 drill test comes along,
Soon it'll be the end of singing the National Anthem on the line,
Or for that matter, any other song.

Now my experience of Sandhurst was different to most, we were there
when Corona struck.
Old College Sunday, cancelled eight hours before it was due to start -
just our luck.
We didn't know it then, but we sure do know it now.
Sandhurst, the bastion of tradition will continue, to our country, its
unwritten vow.

As our time went on, we missed out on a lot of fun.
We longed to escape to London and go to Infernos, but it wasn't to be
the one.
That isn't to say we didn't have hijinks, we undoubtedly did:
As the colour sergeants would say, the biggest crime is getting caught
- so we made sure we hid.

There will be some things I will always remember:

Being by the lake, once the sun had set during a very warm September;
The shout of 'POST' down the corridor was always a highlight;
Sneaking around the ground during the hours of twilight.
Senior Term inflatables on Upper Lake, watching them float around;
Singing "I vow to thee my country" in the Chapel, a roaring and
unforgettable sound.
Having food with international cadets and hearing stories of back home.
Through this momentous journey, nobody was ever alone.

Before you know it, you'll be marching up those steps.
Take all those photos, maybe even keep a diary.
One day, you'll look back without any regrets.

Ed Dawson
Second Lieutenant
Royal Corps of Signals

40 Years

When I first joined in '81
To see the world and have some fun
We lived in times when boys and girls
Inhabited quite different worlds.

So join with me to look at how
So much has changed from then till now;
Old times when expectation was
Girls made the coffee for the boss.

We needed firstly to be trained;
Nine weeks would do it, they explained.
For ladies with some will and vision
To gain themselves a Queens' commission.

While off to Sandhurst, men all went
To 'Ladybird College' gals were sent.
As guys ran round, climbed ropes and towers,
We learned about arranging flowers!

They covered how we should behave;
"Demurely" was advice they gave;
And if we were to have appeal,
We must don make-up and high heels.

And when we joined the guys for lessons
We saw the slide deck presentations
And how they kept the lads' attention
With nudity I blush to mention.

'Twas 40 years since girls had marched
'Longside the men, our kit all starched,
But now we couldn't keep the pace:
Our narrow skirts were like a brace!

The papers said there were no qualms
That women could now carry arms.
We asked "Please may we have a try?"
"That was just for the press," they cried!

We never groused about our pay,
We just earned less; it was the way.
If serving wives chose to conceive
They had no option but to leave.

And women at the front? Hell, no!
Beyond 'Corps Rear' we may not go.
Back then no combat role for 'WRACs'
Just rules that stopped us in our tracks.

At dinner nights, it's true not fable,
Women had to leave the table
So men could share the latest joke
Engulfed in swirling cigar smoke.

It couldn't, though, have been all bad,
This world that clearly favoured lads
Three years was what I signed up for
Then stayed another 24!

And though we have some way to go,
Our women now just simply show
Their level-headed common sense,
                Their courage and resilience.

            They're in all missions far and wide,
            They're at the front and fight 'longside;
            They go unaided to the Pole
            And step up into every role.

            So then as we look back and gaze,
            We see how far we've come and praise
            All those who've helped this come to pass,
            And to them all we raise a glass!

                            Gilly Moncur
                                Veteran
                    Lieutenant Colonel
            Royal Army Educational Corps
                        Army Cadet Force

Unit Life

I'm Not from Anywhere

"Your accent isn't local,
Where are you from?"
I'm not from anywhere.
"Everyone is from somewhere…
Where are you from?"

I'm from Summers playing with kids on the patch;
Clothed in 'thrift shop.'
Pocket money splurged in the NAAFI;
Sat next to my friend on the plane back to school,
Trunk too heavy at Luton Airport

I'm from 110 sleeps till Dad gets back;
Random gifts from the Brunei jungle;
Parties next door; kids sleeping under the table;
Barbeques in the road;
Houses with attics and with cellars.

I'm from a home full of objects from around the globe;
Uniforms hung in every wardrobe.
Dad taught me to iron, not my Mum.
I polished my own shoes on my first day of school,
The first day of every one of my schools.

I'm standing at the altar; I know what I'm doing,
Another child from nowhere at the front of our minds.
How lucky they will be: how lucky I was.
I'm from where I choose, and I wouldn't change it.
I'm not from anywhere.

Sarah McEntee
Captain
Army Cadet Force
Daughter, Wife & Mum of a service family

B.L.A.S.T

Zermatt, a swiss town locked in our hearts,
Army ladies race training camp, in a land far apart.
Girls from different Regiments ready to go,
With Coaches Andy B & his sidekick Dobo.

Bright starts on the glacier,
Early morning chill,
With high speed Giant Slalom turns,
Learning a brand new skill.

Afternoons spent running and lifting heavy weights,
A bit of sunbathing thrown in to help rejuvenate.
Friday nights out- did we let off steam!
A good knees up required, with fancy dress sometimes the theme.

The Brown Cow, Spitfire and Broken Barrels,
Favourite spots to have one or two jars.
Dancing on the tables by the end of the night,
Giving the locals a proper fright.

We definitely had our day,
And blew the RAF and Navy away.
The following year, new racers appear.

We swooped to clinch a second win!
Combined services team victory.
Army was the team that took the win.

With Andy and Dobo's early starts up on the hill,
Working the team tirelessly developing their skills.
Not forgetting Paul, the Manager and financial man supreme,
Who with all the girls formed one very special team.

Andy Brown
Veteran
Staff Sergeant
Royal Corps of Signals

On Patrol

It's your turn for patrol, kid, get up, get ready!
Check your weapons, check your equipment,
Slip on your bulletproof vest,
With two slabs of bullet-stopping material.

It's patrol from an army Land Rover APV,
So, strap on your helmet, clean the visor from the last patrol,
Scraping off food waste, and sometimes other waste…
We're not always everyone's saviour.

Out on patrol, chatting and joking with your team,
Brick commander issuing orders.
You deploy from the vehicle, get into your designated order.
Last man is your six, checking behind for danger.
Everyone tense, knowing there could be trouble at any time.

It's two in the morning, you're off patrol, the NAAFI closed.
You stash your weapons and equipment,
Head for the mess hall and cheap bread, white of course,
And tray upon tray of eggs.
What did Edwina Currie know?
Bet she never came off patrol

The egg banjo was calling…
Getting the brews on, two coffees and two teas.

Debrief time:
Not before the usual discussion: red, brown or no sauce at all?
Come on! It has to be red!
Time for bed.
Ready for another patrol in four hours.
It's like a scene from The Waltons.
We all wish each other goodnight.
The one thing you have is respect for one another.
The team.
Each holding the others' lives in your hands.
Brothers till the end.

Ian Humpleby
Veteran
Guardsman
Coldstream Guards

Cyprus

My first posting was to Germany,
Which soon became my new homeground.
It felt like the north of England,
But with foreigners around.
Then I was posted out to Cyprus,
And I quickly fell in love,
With its sandy golden beaches,
And a raging sun high up above.

The food was just amazing,
For a lad brought up on chips,
Fresh salads with huge tomatoes,
That took inches from my hips.
People, warm and friendly,
With smiles spread on each face.
Weather always sunny,
Made me love this magic place.

Then all too soon I had to go,
Back to the cold and damp.
Living in our married quarter,
On a chilly English camp.
But there's something deep inside me,
Keeps me warm while we're apart.
For there's a little bit of Cyprus,
That I carry in my heart.

Clive Sanders
Veteran
Captain
Royal Corps of Signals

Operations

East Timor

It's 0900 hours and the sun is
high and hot.
I stand here watching,
I stand here listening.
What was once chaos, now is not!

The waves roll in and crash down,
It's now the only sound around.
The view of golden sands and deep blue sea.
Once a place of tragedy,
Now a place of tranquility.

Yet I stand here, armed
With my gun.
    I stand here ready.
        This peaceful place.
            Turned back to what it once was not.

Gina Allsop
Veteran
Sergeant
Royal Corps of Signals

Simply Me

It might have been me - taken by the sea.
Perhaps it should have been me?

I suffer pain, physically and mentally,
every day of my life.
Is this a punishment for me?
Many years I lost - not knowing who is me?

As I allowed myself to be consumed with a
life without connections to the sea.
In those years I helped nurture my
children, to beyond my own shortcomings,
beyond being me.
I'm ok with it not being me - taken by
the sea.

Now I have reconnected with friends of
old,
I remember what it was like to be me.
Knowing who was lost to the sea, I
still feel guilt that it wasn't
me.

But my family needed me, and
my business releases me. So, I
salute those taken by the sea.
Though I did not know you all,
you are still brothers to me.

I will live the rest of my
days knowing it wasn't me
taken by the sea.

Russ Kirby
Veteran
Seaman
Royal Navy

Battlefield

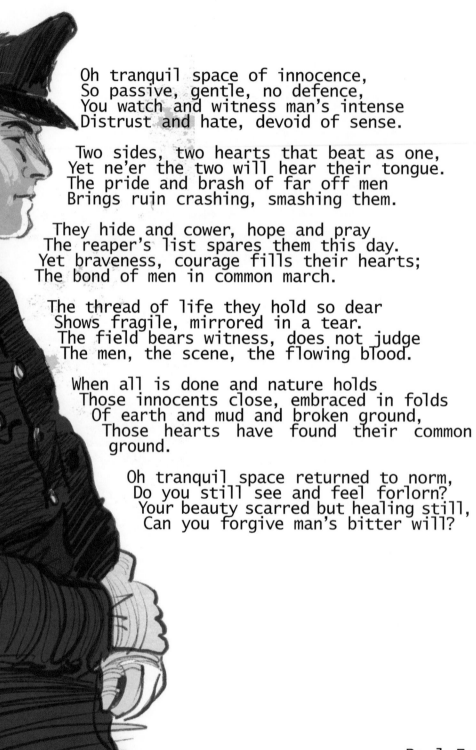

Oh tranquil space of innocence,
So passive, gentle, no defence,
You watch and witness man's intense
Distrust and hate, devoid of sense.

Two sides, two hearts that beat as one,
Yet ne'er the two will hear their tongue.
The pride and brash of far off men
Brings ruin crashing, smashing them.

They hide and cower, hope and pray
The reaper's list spares them this day.
Yet braveness, courage fills their hearts;
The bond of men in common march.

The thread of life they hold so dear
Shows fragile, mirrored in a tear.
The field bears witness, does not judge
The men, the scene, the flowing blood.

When all is done and nature holds
Those innocents close, embraced in folds
Of earth and mud and broken ground,
Those hearts have found their common
ground.

Oh tranquil space returned to norm,
Do you still see and feel forlorn?
Your beauty scarred but healing still,
Can you forgive man's bitter will?

Paul Ford
Veteran
Major
Royal Corps of Signals

Capt Chavasse VC

Here, son – it's rum;
When you're in Hell – so what?
Tomorrow we'll see the sun,
And this nightmare will be brought to naught.

The Highlands are far away
But your family is still there.
Tomorrow you will see your bray
And they will have your loss to bear.

But you and I will walk again.
At home, for me Liverpool – but for you,
The glens in the falling rain.
For me, the Liver Birds will call.

John Jessop
Veteran
Major
Royal Army Educational Corps

Home at Last

He's home at last, a mother's son, a fine young man, his duty done.
Yet not for him the fond embrace, a loving kiss, a smiling face,
Or cries of joy to laugh and cheer the safe return of one so dear.
It is his lot to show the world a soldier's fate, as flags unfurl
And Standards lower in salutation, symbols of a grateful nation.

Sombre now, the drum beats low, as he is carried, gentle, so
As if not to disturb his rest, by comrades, three and three abreast,
Who now, as quiet orders sound, they, one by one then move around
To place him in the carriage decked with flowers in calm and hushed respect,
Preparing for the sad, slow ride through silent crowds who wait outside.

So, the warrior now returns
to native soil and rightly earns
The great respect to one so young,
though sadness stills the waiting throng,
While flowers strew the path he takes, as the carriage slowly makes
A final turning to allow the veterans standing there to show
The soldier's pride, a silent, mute, proud and respectful last salute.

Yet, while onlookers stand and see the simple, moving ceremony,
There is a home, a place somewhere, where sits a waiting, vacant chair,
And one great yawning empty space in someone's heart, no last embrace
To bid a final, fond farewell to one who will forever dwell
In love and cherished memory, a husband, son, eternally.

And we who see should not forget that in this soldier's final debt,
And sacrifice for duty's sake, it is the loved ones who must take
The hurt, to bear as best they can, and face a future lesser than
The one they dreamed in bygone years.
Now to regard with bitter tears,
Reflecting, as time intervenes,
On thoughts of how it might have been.

But in their grief there's quiet pride that loved ones bravely fought and died,
Believing in a worthy goal which helps give solace, and consoles
By knowing that the loss they bear is shared by all our people
Where in gratitude, their names will be forever honoured, guaranteed
To be remembered and enshrined,
Beyond the shifting sands of time.

Tony Church
Veteran
Corporal
Royal Electrical & Mechanical Engineers

Leaving the Forces

The Black Dog*

Do not let the black dog bite you,
Do not be or feel afraid.

Make it walk alongside you,
And watch the shadow begin to fade.

Ted Granger
Veteran
Royal Air Force

*The Black Dog is the name Winston Churchill gave to the deep depression he often
suffered from.

In Touch

Thoughts of trials, challenges and the unknown
With those who frame your highs and lows.
The hopes and fears of every day,
Trying to be the thing 'they' want.

Discipline, resilience and friendship come
With shared experience and reliance.
The trepidation of the unknown,
Tempered by the family bond.

With those I served, remain the strongest
Bonds of friendship, kinship and trust.
For only they know where we journeyed,
Mentally, physically, spiritually.

Age brings changes and deeper knowledge,
And as life spreads the miles apart,
Always the connection is there,
To keep the ties that make us 'we'.

Mogs Southern
Veteran
Major
Royal Corps of Signals

Me

My name is Tommy; this is about me,
And how I struggle with PTSD,
So welcome one and welcome all,
For us soldiers, it's a masquerade ball.

As we put on our masks, just for one night,
We try to put aside our worries and fright,
This prison I live in is deep in my brain,
What is going on? I feel totally insane.

This prison's my home and where I reside,
I have nowhere to run; nowhere to hide.
Every decision I'm questioning me,
What is this illness called PTSD?

What's going on? Why do I feel like I do?
Someone explain 'cos I haven't a clue.
Look at me now; you can see nothing wrong,
Mentally this has been going on too long.

No scars on my body; no wounds to find,
All of my injuries etched on my mind.
No signs of injury; no signs of pain,
Flashbacks and nightmares over and over again.

But with Help for Heroes, help was a must,
I built up the courage, friendship and trust.
Look at me now, standing tall, feeling proud,
In front of a friendly, heart-warming crowd.

So now I say thank you for all that you've done,
I don't have to fight with a bayonet and gun,
As with your help this fight's practically won,
Thanks Help for Heroes, my wife, daughter and son

My name is Tommy; this was about me
And how I now handle my PTSD.

Tommy Lowther
Veteran
Private
Light Infantry
Founder & CEO of Sporting Force

My Life with PTSD

The chaos in my life,
The battle in my brain,
The need to have someone,
Take away the pain.

I'm fed up fighting now,
But I never will give in,
Life is so very special,
To lose it would be a sin.

I am sad and scared, "quite frightened",
Of what is ahead, in store,
There has got to be some peace,
That is what I'm yearning for.

I have to come to realise this,
While at COMBAT STRESS,
The only way to freedom,
Is to clean up my own mess.

Stop moaning, blaming others,
Feeling sorry for myself,
STOP USING BOOZE AS THE ANSWER,
Forget that old top shelf.

Only I can set me free,
So many more have tried,
I must move on, get a life,
Must turn back the bloody tide.

I KNOW IT WILL NOT BE EASY,
LOTS OF MATES HAVE DIED,
But I will always remember them,
For them I've already cried.

It's for them I live in memory,
For them I carry on,
It is what they would have wanted,
Stop being weak: be strong!

SO HERE TO YOU I PROMISE,
To fight this day by day,
That small ray of hope, that ray of sunshine,
That grows inside me today.

To carry on, to be a man,
TO DO MY VERY BEST.
HAVE A SMILE, DO SOME GOOD,
AND LET GOD DO THE REST !

Paul Percival
Veteran
Royal Marine Commando
Royal Marines

Cenotaph

I've lived my life, I've had great fun, even lost my temper.
I served my Queen, in a brotherhood, I always shall remember!
During that time, I drank some beer, enough to kill a whale!
I've eaten things, many would not, and marched all through the
hail!
One thing I learned, from that great life, was the meaning of true
friend!
You'd watch his back, and he watched yours, his was mine to defend!

In days gone past, many did fight, in far, far distant land,
With mortar, rifle, grenade and bomb, even hand to hand!
It's because of these souls who fought for us, that we are all now
free,
To laugh, to joke, to holiday, and go on a shopping spree!
My grandad was just but one, of Britain's fine brave men!
Who went to fight the tyrant foe! We must remember them!

Our brave were sent, across this world, to honour and defend!
They fought so fearless, they fought real hard, many to their end!
The list of killed and wounded ones, is an impossibly great number,
Many lives lost carelessly, because of some fool's blunder!
Yet still they went to fight the war, striking a deadly blow!
Many now in cemeteries, lined up, row on row!

I was lucky, for I march on, now I live a life so different.
Yes, the faces of my fallen friends,
will never be too distant!
I raise a glass this time of year!
I remember all they've done!
I remember those just left behind!
Once they'd buried their son.
So my suit is cleaned, my beret
shaped, and yes I'm sure to laugh!
But I'll shed a tear with my warrior
clan, as we march past the Cenotaph!

Stu Mears
Veteran
Corporal
Princess of Wales Royal Regiment

Loss

The day you went
The sun forgot to shine

The day you went
The clouds began to thicken

The day you went
The rain began to pour

The day you went
The thunder cracked and roared

The day you went
The ground was soaked and the world went grey

An then, in time a Rainbow shone through
To remind me of the wonders of you.

Gina Allsop
Veteran
Sergeant
Royal Corps of Signals
Army Cadet Force

Aged

Eyes have greyed, but not dimmed.
Straight proud backs, long since bowed.
Strength is in heart and mind, but less in muscle.
Marching on with determination but more in shuffle.
The few get fewer, leaving ever more empty tables.

Once a year jaws set firm;
Iron those creases sharp,
Shine worn shoes,
Polish precious metal:
Deep breath, step forth.

Bugle sound, painful silence;
Bowed becomes straight, eyes so clear.
Drums, beat, march.
Trample of the few, ranks swelled by the long since silent.
None forgotten, all missed.

Return to favoured pasture,
Speeches aplenty, drinks all around, arms on shoulders strong.
Rolls of honour, ever longer, pride of place.
Memories flow, then becomes now, laughter, friends, comrades, tears!
Melancholy strikes the hour, this year is ending.
Backs to bow, shuffle now, home!
Mark time, wait, watch, hope…

Tony Carr
Veteran
Sergeant
Royal Artillery
Army Cadet Force

Beauty

A soulmate filled with passion,
A spirit alive with grace,
The figure of a goddess
Beneath an angel's face.

All life she does embellish,
The eternal world's bright sun,
A stunning quest for perfection
I've found in you as one.

Mark Thomas
Veteran
Rifleman
Royal Green Jackets

Enjoy

We're springer spaniels
And we love to walk.
Can't ask to go out though,
Because we can't talk.

So we get excited
And watch every move.
Boots, towels, and leads
Is what we approve.

When we are asked
We'll leap in the car.
Don't care where we go
But hope that it's far
And hope we get out of the car.
To explore Yorkshire's land
Cos car rides and walkies
Just go hand in hand.
We might end up
In Round Howe or Reeth.
Chase squirrels and rabbits
Although they've got big teeth!
Plantation or Gallops
We don't really mind.
Our noses get busy
There's dead animals to find!

We love the water
And we love the mud.
Don't care if it's raining,
Not bothered by flood
Not bothered by wind
Or bothered by snow.

And we remember the sand
From so long ago.
Please take us back
To the beaches in Thanet.
We know that you will
But you just can't plan it.

We love the river
We'll ramble the hills.
And our canine friends
Provide pleasant thrills.
Cos we get so bored

And lonely at home,
If we're given the chance
We'll happily roam.

And when we get back,
All cold, wet and muddy,
We'll get rubbed down,
And sometimes the hose.

Left to dry off,
While she changed her clothes.
We jumped up and shook,
And we shared our dirty
Muddy paw prints
Over her jeans and shirt.

So, we don't really care
When walking's our right,
Provoking our dreams
So we howl in the night.

When you pick up our leads
And your car keys jangle,
This surely will help
The stress disentangle.
So watch us running,

Chasing through grass,
And take us out now!
Get off of your arse!
We need more walkies.

It calms us right down,
Fresh air and freedom.
Prevents the meltdown.
We need to get out.
We need to get tired.
We need our dog life,

It's certainly required
To make us real happy.
Our purpose is play,
And something we need
To do everyday.

We're springer spaniels
Thanks for your time.
We hoped you enjoyed
Our cute little rhyme!

Sue Cross
Veteran
Warrant Officer First Class
Adjutant General's Corps

My Hand!

My hand. It learns to play
A guitar in school, and maybe a flute one day.

My hand. It fires a rifle today,
It learns to aim and hit a target far away, far away!

My hand. It is injured from an op gone astray.
It's cut open, repaired, perhaps, they say.

My hand. It's Ok, had worse, who am I to complain?
But it wears now a lovely ring; a pledge to remain.

My hand. It is in pain, most days.
The hand I see every day.

My hand. Is it my hand?
It has stories to tell, and things it could say.

Gina Allsop
Veteran
Sergeant
Royal Corps of Signals
Army Cadet Force

The Forces Family

I am a Mum

I love my son, I am his mum!
I am so proud and amazed at all he has done.
It was so scary when he joined the Forces;
His aim was good, and he made amazing choices.

Samaritans and mental health awareness have become his special role,
But to care and support are special emotions for such a special soul.
To look after those who struggle to see,
How well they have done, and how great they can be.

He is my son, and I am his mum.
So, so proud of all he has done!

Barbara Crosthwaite
Mum of RAF Officer

Sister

My baby sister - a tomboy at heart.
Hardly surprising the career she would start.

Fresh faced - Just nineteen.
Ready and waiting to serve country and Queen.

Enlisted! The Signals!
It all happened so fast.

Posting began
Bluies came at last.

They told of adventure, of travel, of laughter,
Her friendships;
Don't mention location, trauma, will writing,
Her censorship.

Whilst decking the halls one Christmas Eve night.
A knock on the door - our best gift alright!
Our sister, Mum's daughter, their auntie,
Her life.

Eleven years past, at last she would leave.
Decorated with medals,
For service to all,
To country, to Queen.

She continues to serve through her charity work,
Caring for animals, nature, our Earth.

More apparent with age,
The pace and the pain,
On her body, her brain.
In fly SSAFA!
Supporting with grace,
In the shape of a bike
For her charity race.

So thankful to have her.
Sadly, too many sisters have not been so blessed.
My sister, I love her.
She is the BEST!

Kim Gregory
Sister of a British Army soldier

Just Me and the Ocean

It is just me.
Me and the vast ocean.
Nothing. And everything.
Holding me. I feel weightless.
The gentle, constant stroke of the water
Soothing my soul.

I rock side to side
Raising my arms over head
Catching the water and seeing the bubbles
Deftly escaping my fingers
Power and strength, as the water and I meet in embrace.
I push, and roll.

All I see is dark blue. And me.
The long arm and hand stretched out
Each stroke a move towards the unknown vast of ocean.
I breathe.
The land a steady rock
The colours of beach huts dance across my eyes
The blue sky winks and reminds me:

Right now, all my worries, there is nothing I can do.
But swim.
All is well with the world.
It is just me.
Me and the vast ocean.

Verity Green
Partner of Royal Navy Serviceman
Former H4H volunteer

Small

When I awake and go to school
I sometimes think of how I'm small.
And when I reach up and face the teacher's stare
I sometimes think that life's unfair.

But when the bell rings and it's not the phone
It's time to end, it's time for home.
I brush my hair and my beret I don;
My friends and I, we're marching on.

I often smile, as its fun for free
My life and world, it's No 3.
But out of class and out of school
I'm a cadet and I'm nine feet tall.

Blake Baxendale
Cadet Lance Corporal
Army Cadet Force

Somewhere to Run

From the pain, from the glass,
The pointless exercise and after class,
The moment of life and the smell of tea,
The sight of Dad and need to flee.
But this is the night
That I can go
To the safest place, only I know.

The smell of stores and army scent,
The NAAFI shillings that I have spent,
The woolly pully and gaiter smell,
The Sergeant Major who came from hell.
But he was my brother, my father and all.
That was the place that had the pull,
My mates from the street,
The mates from school.

All cadets are mates in arms,
The very people who ran from harm.
The weekend camps and the 303,
The time away, no need to flee,
Metal mugs and crappy food,
A slap for snitching or being rude.
But when the fun ends and it's time for home.

I'll be thinking of where there's a need to roam.
At least on Monday it's Army Cadet time,
Stand tall and proud and stand in line.
It's only a day, or is it two?
But it'll always be heaven,
The place to run to.

Tim Scargill
Sergeant Instructor
Army Cadet Force
Poem Written in 1972 when Tim was a cadet.

The Volunteer

When I was young, I was shy and afraid.
A friend said "Join cadets! It's different every day."
So I joined.
My back was curled,
My eyes to the floor,
But with every parade night I felt myself stand tall.

I was shown respect,
And only asked for courage in return.
I gained passion, self-belief and pride,
But after 18 years I had to leave on the next tide.

A decade passed until I returned,
To give back all that I had learned
Of duty, passion, honour and pride,
The values & standards that stayed by my side.

Ten years a CFAV
My job is not done:
Still there is work to do;
As long as my heart beats, cadets' will do too.

To see a cadet grow from child to young adult,
To gain respect, loyalty, integrity
And to witness their selfless commitment,
As a CFAV it reinforces our motto
And my belief that we should all

'Inspire to achieve'

Katie Tarrant
Sergeant Major Instructor
Army Cadet Force

One Life Lost

One life lost, many more to go
Before we forget who's friend or foe

The life of one means nothing to some,
But the family of whom, they cry

Sending their son,
To the battle we won,
Not knowing they'll surely die

But in that solemn silence
That ended all the violence
Is a whisper of a cacophony

War, bloodshed, and torment
Reincarnated as a poppy.

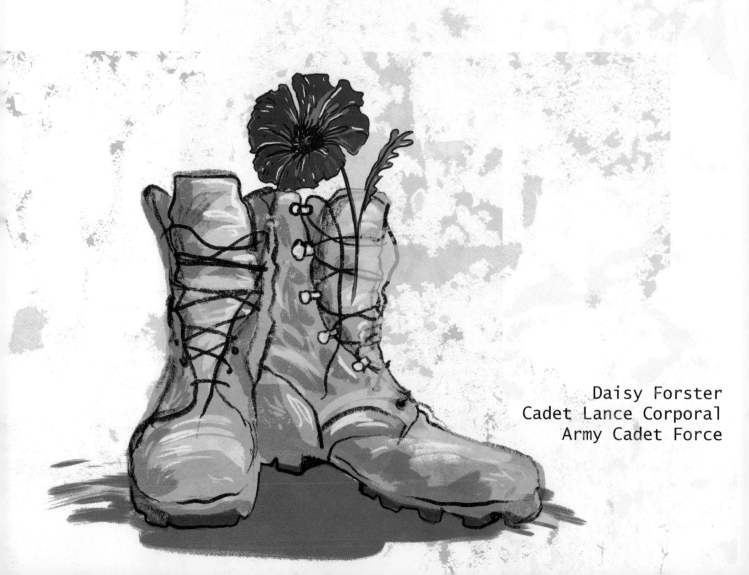

Daisy Forster
Cadet Lance Corporal
Army Cadet Force

Passing Stranger

Passing stranger,
dancing child,
here, in our shadow,
rest ... for a while.
You won't know me...
yet heed me well...
mine was a story
pray you'll never tell...
scripted by many hands,
but ended alone...

Written in blood...
carved in stone.

Passing stranger,
dancing child,
here, in our shadow,
light up your smile...
Your lips ... softly
voice our names;
there...
in your whispering,
we live
again.

See us all marching still,
line after line...
Please remember us
from time...

...to time.

Steve O'Kane
Brother of a Royal Artillery Solider